IDA TARBELL
Pioneer Investigative Reporter

IDA TARBELL
Pioneer Investigative Reporter

Barbara A. Somervill

MORGAN
REYNOLDS
Publishers, Inc.

620 South Elm Street, Suite 223
Greensboro, North Carolina 27406
http://www.morganreynolds.com

IDA TARBELL: PIONEER INVESTIGATIVE REPORTER

Library of Congress Cataloging-in-Publication Data

Somervill, Barbara A.
    Ida Tarbell : pioneer investigative reporter / Barbara A. Somervill.
        p. cm. -- (World writers)
    Includes bibliographical references and index.
    Summary: Follows the life of Ida Tarbell, from her childhood among the oil fields of
    western Pennsylvania through her career as a biographer and investigative journalist.
    ISBN 1-883846-87-0 (lib. bdg.)
        1. Tarbell, Ida M. (Ida Minerva), 1857-1944--Juvenile literature. 2. Journalists--United
    States--Biography--Juvenile literature. [1. Tarbell, Ida M. (Ida Minerva), 1857-1944. 2.
    Journalists. 3. Women--Biography.] I. Title. II. Series.

PN4874.T23 S66 2002
070.92--dc21
[B]
                                                                    2001058727

For Chuck—I couldn't do it without you.

Contents

Ida M. Tarbell
(Library of Congress)

Chapter One

A Curious Mind

Some children are simply born curious—Ida Tarbell was one of them. The brook that ran by her childhood home intrigued her. She noticed that some things floated on the water, while other things sank to the bottom. Young Ida spent hours tossing in twigs, stones, and leaves, and watching the results.

Interested to find out if her brother was a "floater" or a "sinker," four-year-old Ida led her younger brother, Will, to the footbridge over the brook and tossed him in the water. In the 1860s, toddlers wore dresses, and the skirts of young Will Tarbell's dress held him up. Of course, he screamed in fright. A man working nearby rushed to Will's rescue. Ida was delighted. Will was a "floater."

Late in life, Ida recalled "the peace of satisfied curiosity" in completing her first scientific experiment. Will, the subject of this first investigation, luckily survived in one piece. Many of those whom Ida investigated in her adulthood did not do quite so well. Under Ida's examination, many proved to be "sinkers."

Ida Minerva Tarbell was born on November 5, 1857, in the log home of her grandparents. Her parents, Franklin Sumner Tarbell and Esther Ann McCullough Tarbell, had married in 1856 and planned to settle in Iowa. Franklin left for Iowa, leaving his wife with her family in Hatch Hollow, Pennsylvania.

The McCullough's log house was not a rustic cabin; rather it was a large, Cape Cod-style home. The floors were made from oak, and a huge fireplace took up most of one wall in the living room.

In 1857, a financial panic closed banks, and the money Franklin planned to use to start his family farm was no longer available to him. He was stuck in Iowa with no money to bring Esther to him or for him to return to Pennsylvania. Esther and her infant daughter were forced to remain with the McCulloughs until Franklin could join them.

With no money in his pocket, Franklin set out on foot for Pennsylvania. He worked on the way as a teacher. By the time he arrived in Hatch Hollow, Ida was already eighteen months old.

The McCullough's farm was always busy and filled with life. As a child, Ida played with ducks and chickens, lambs and calves, and the ever-present kittens and puppies. She often remembered the farm's milk room, "with its dozens of filled [milk] pans on the racks, its huge wooden bowl heaped with yellow butter on its way to the firkin, its baskets piled with eggs, its plump dressed poultry ready for market." For young Ida, this was the ideal home.

When Franklin Tarbell returned to Pennsylvania broke and without a plan to support his young family, the new oil industry gave him hope for the future. For centuries, Native Americans had used oil they found seeping to the surface in present-day Pennsylvania. As early as 1400 AD, local tribes dug small pits around these oil seeps and lined the pits with wood. They harvested the petroleum and used it for lamplight and medicine.

In the 1840s, Pittsburgh's Samuel Kier experimented with crude petroleum. Kier processed the dark, thick oil into a lighter lamp fuel. The fuel burned as well as whale oil, the popular lamp fuel of the time. Kier's fuel was also much cheaper than whale oil. However, gathering oil that had seeped up to the surface was not an effective way to collect the petroleum. A better method of taking the petroleum from inside the earth needed to be found.

In 1859, Edwin Drake drilled an oil well near Titusville, Pennsylvania. Drake hit oil at seventy feet. News of the Drake Well spread like wildfire. Just as miners and prospectors surged to California for the 1849 gold rush, potential oilmen rushed to western Pennsylvania to drill for oil. In a matter of months, wooden derricks dotted the region, oil seeps spotted the land, and a new industry took its first toddling steps.

As oil gushed from wells, quite a bit leaked out

because barrels were not well made. Franklin Tarbell was an experienced carpenter. He suggested to one oilman that he could make a tank that would hold 500 barrels of oil without leaking. The oilman said he would buy Tarbell's tank if what he claimed were true. Franklin proved his tanks were as good as his word and became the local supplier for oil tanks.

Franklin's new business in nearby Rouseville soon prospered, and he was able to build the family a small residence adjacent to his woodshop. The Tarbell's first home away from the McCulloughs consisted of a living room, a kitchen, and a family bedroom. The children— Ida and brother William Walter, who was born in July 1860—slept in trundle beds that were stored under their parents' bed during the daytime. Ida spent hours in the shop, taking naps in the pine shavings and breathing in the crisp smell of freshly cut wood.

Unfortunately, Ida was used to her grandparents' farm and found her life in Rouseville very restrictive. She resented the confinement so much she tried to run away, but only got as far as the hill near her house before turning back.

Ida's mother saw the dangers of living amid oil wells and kept close tabs on Ida's activities. Abandoned derricks loomed high over earth puddled with oil and sludge. There were deep oil pits into which a child could fall unnoticed. A thin coat of petroleum covered the trees, shrubs, and ground. Even the air that they breathed smelled of oil. There was always danger amidst the thrill of gushers, spouters, and boundless wealth.

A typical Pennsylvania oil field, 1865.
(Library of Congress)

Once, disaster struck close to the Tarbell's home when neighbor Henry Rouse was drilling for oil. As the well came in, oil shot out in a fountain over the top of the derrick. By accident, a light ignited the natural gas that escaped with the oil. A massive explosion thundered throughout the town. Rouse and eighteen men burned to death.

Late that night, one of the survivors stumbled to the Tarbells' door. Burned beyond recognition, this man could barely give his name before he collapsed. The Tarbells sitting room became a clinic. For months, Esther Tarbell's spotless parlor smelled of linseed oil and medicines as Esther nursed the injured man back to health.

Another time, a neighbor poured oil on the wood in her cookstove to help light the fire, clearly unaware of the danger. However, live coals in the firebox ignited, exploding in the kitchen. The woman and two friends died in the fire. Although forbidden to see the burned bodies, curious, eight-year-old Ida could not restrain herself. She sneaked into the room where the women were laid out for burial. One glimpse of the burned bodies gave Ida nightmares that would follow her throughout her life.

Beyond the reaches of the Oil Region, the United States was undergoing drastic changes. After the election of Abraham Lincoln as president, many Southern states left the Union to form the Confederate States of America. In April 1861, the Civil War began when Confederates fired shots on Federal Fort Sumter on the South Carolina coast. Southern leaders felt threatened by Lincoln's promise to limit the spread of slavery.

The Tarbell family subscribed to *Harper's Weekly, Harper's Monthly,* and the *New York Tribune.* These magazines were frequently the only means of getting news. Ida and her brother Will followed the events of the Civil War through magazine articles. They poured over news of battles, numbers of wounded and dead, and the actions of Generals Grant, Sherman, and McClellan. President Lincoln stated throughout the war: "My paramount object in the struggle is to save the Union." In 1862, Lincoln freed slaves in all Southern states through the Emancipation Proclamation.

The Civil War ended with the surrender of Robert E.

Lee on April 9, 1865 at Appomattox Courthouse, Virginia. Five days later, John Wilkes Booth shot and killed President Lincoln at Ford's Theater in Washington, D.C.

On the day the news reached Rouseville, Ida's father came home early from work, his head hung low, his step slow and measured. Esther ran to meet him, and buried her tear-stained face in her apron upon learning that Abraham Lincoln was dead. Black crape hung over the doors as the country mourned the loss of its leader.

Death was not limited to war and oil accidents. The Tarbell family had expanded with the births of Sarah and Franklin, Jr. Unfortunately, scarlet fever struck both younger children at an early age. Eleven-year-old Ida stood helpless and white-knuckled outside Frankie's door, as her youngest brother screamed from the pain of his illness. Frankie died, and Sarah remained physically weak for much of her life. From then on, Ida always panicked whenever Will or Sarah became ill.

By 1869, wells in Rouseville and strikes in nearby Pithole had played out. Where oil remained, iron tanks replaced the wooden ones built by Franklin Tarbell. It was time to move on, and the Tarbells headed to Titusville, the cultural center of western Pennsylvania, where Franklin would begin drilling oil on his own.

With a population of 10,000, Titusville offered many things that smaller Rouseville did not. There were sidewalks and sewers, churches, banks, and a local newspaper. The Tarbells attended the Methodist Church at least twice a week. A police force kept order, and schools provided education for the town's children. On the sidewalks, organ grinders played music for the passing crowds. At night, gas lamps lit the streets.

Nearby Pithole plunged from boom to bust, leaving behind empty buildings and abandoned wells. Franklin Tarbell saw opportunity in Pithole's defeat. He purchased the vacant Bonta Hotel—originally built for $60,000—for only $600. From the hotel's lumber, ornaments, and windows, Franklin built his family a two-story house with a tower on Main Street, Titusville.

The boom and bust cycle of the oil industry worried some, such as Standard Oil founder John D. Rockefeller. A shrewd businessman, Rockefeller saw the fluctuations of the industry as inefficient. His dream was to control the entire oil business: drilling, refining, transportation, and sales. Rockefeller's Standard Oil Company began to buy out small refineries in the Oil Region and soon controlled most of the refineries there.

In 1871, the South Improvement Company (SIC) arrived to burst the financial bubble of small, independent oil companies, like Franklin Tarbell's. The South Improvement Company was a secret alliance between the Pennsylvania Railroad and several large oil companies, including Standard Oil. The SIC pact was simple. The railroad raised its rates for shipping oil, and SIC oil companies would receive rebates against their rates, saving them money. Independent oil companies paid the high rates, but would get no rebate money.

Independent oilmen like Tarbell could not compete against budding giants like Standard Oil in either refining or shipping. They could not afford to sell their kerosene, paraffin, or petroleum products as cheaply as Standard Oil. They had only two choices: sell or rebel.

The South Improvement Company and Standard Oil became Ida Tarbell's arch enemies. She watched as the oil monopoly, like a massive python, squeezed the life from the Oil Region. Her father changed from a gentle man to a vigilante. Franklin and other Titusville independents tipped over railroad tankers filled with Standard Oil crude. The angry oilmen marched through town carrying torches and terrorizing SIC and Standard Oil agents.

The independents pleaded with the U.S. Congress to help them while they held out against Standard Oil and the Pennsylvania Railroad. Within a year, the Pennsylvania government disbanded the South Improvement Company. In the Oil Region, independents considered the end of the SIC a triumph. For Rockefeller, it was meaningless. He was deeply involved in buying up competitive oil companies in the Cleveland area.

Fair or not, Ida believed her father and family suffered because of the sly business practices of one man–John D. Rockefeller. Little did Rockefeller realize that the SIC created a lifelong enemy who would eventually topple his empire.

Chapter Two

Knowledge and Independence

Ida's mother, Esther, was a staunch supporter of women's rights, and for many years, nationally-known temperance leaders, crusaders, and independent thinkers had visited the Tarbells. One such visit stood out to Ida's mind. When Ida was a teenager, her mother was visited by Mary Rice Livermore, founder of the Illinois Women's Suffrage Association, and Frances E. Willard, who began the Women's Christian Temperance Union. Although the women were fighting for the futures of young girls like Ida, Ida remembers feeling overlooked by the reformers. She wrote later: "I remember best Mary Livermore and Frances Willard—not that either touched me, saw me, of this neglect I was acutely conscious. I noted too that the men we entertained did notice me, talked to me as a person and not merely as a possible member of a society they were promoting." Although Ida appreciated some of the aspects of the women's movement, she would never become a strong supporter, believing that both men and women were guilty of being unfair to each other.

That is not to say that Ida overlooked such unfairness in her own home. She noted that her well-educated, capable mother had given up her teaching career once she married. Ida also was aware that while her mother was responsible for maintaining the household, buying food and clothing, and managing expenses, Esther never really knew how much money was available for the family. Men earned and controlled the money; women had to guess how much could be spent to keep the household running smoothly. Ida became determined to have more control over her own life.

While living in Rouseville, Ida had attended a small, intimate school where the teacher, Mrs. Rice, befriended her. Once the family moved to Titusville, Ida discovered school was quite different from the friendly, homey atmosphere she enjoyed as a child.

In Titusville, Ida was just one of many students in the class. In an act of petty rebellion, Ida skipped school, thinking no one would know or care. She was wrong. One day Mary French, Ida's teacher, scolded Ida for wasting her intelligence and disgracing her parents by her behavior. Stunned, Ida immediately changed her ways and applied herself, eventually rising to the top of her class.

Ida studied science, geography, history, English grammar, rhetoric, and writing. Above all else, Ida reveled in science. Frogs, rocks, leaves, and bugs fascinated her. From her early childhood, Ida had gathered abandoned birds' nests, interesting minerals, and leaves from plants she found in the Pennsylvania woodland. Now, she had a reason for collecting her specimens.

Ida had heard of Darwin and his theories on the origin of life. His book *Origin of Species* that explained his theory of natural selection had been published in 1859. Ida moved herself and her collections into the tower room, where she set up a microscope. She set her mind to uncovering the workings of evolution, although the theory contradicted her family's Methodist beliefs.

Thrilled by the opportunity science opened to her, and discouraged by the limited roles open to married women, Ida set two goals for herself. First, she would become a microscopist and, second, she would never marry. For a person with the inborn curiosity and intelligence Ida possessed, college would be the key to a new world.

In 1876, Ida entered Allegheny College in Meadville, Pennsylvania. Founded in 1815 and associated with the United Methodist Church, Allegheny College had only recently begun accepting female students. At the time of Ida's enrollment, she was the only woman in her class, and one of only seven female students in the school.

In those days, Allegheny was comprised of three buildings: Bentley Hall, Culver Hall, and Ruter Hall. Bentley was where classes were held, Culver was a men's dormitory, and Ruter housed the school's library. According to Ida, "If Bentley Hall . . . was a beautiful piece of architecture, its interior could hardly have been more severe. The rooms were heated with potbellied cast-iron stoves, seated with the hardest wooden chairs, lighted by kerosene lamps. In winter . . . snow tracked in kept the floors wet and cold. Often one wore a muffler in chapel."

Despite the physical hardships, Ida found her classes challenging and exciting. One professor in particular—Jeremiah Tingley—encouraged her interest in science. Tingley was a lively, dedicated teacher. Once he discovered Ida's interest in the microscope, he offered to let her use the high-powered scope in the science labs.

One of Ida's first scientific investigations at Allegheny was studying what she called "the missing link." This creature was a mud puppy. Just over a foot long, the animal had both a lung and gills. It was slimy, revolting, and thoroughly fascinating. Ida spent much of her free time trying to prove the theory of evolution in her investigation of the mud puppy. Ida described her dedication to science later: "The quest for the truth had been born in me . . . the most essential of man's quests."

Professor Tingley refused to let his students isolate themselves from the rest of the world. He was interested in inventions and advances of all kinds. Tingley learned that at the Centennial Exposition of 1876, Alexander Graham Bell was presenting his telephone to the world. Ida attended the Centennial Exposition with her father and brother, but missed Bell's exhibit. When she returned to college from the exposition, Tingley asked her all about the telephone, but Ida knew nothing of it. Tingley expressed his disappointment. He correctly predicted that the telephone would connect people from distant cities, allowing them to talk from New York to Boston—a radical idea at the time.

Ida's four years at Allegheny College passed quickly. Upon graduation, she accepted the job of preceptress, or headmistress, of Poland Union Seminary in Poland, Ohio. For her teaching Ida earned a $500 yearly salary. She was delighted with both the job and the salary. The first because it was a respected position; the second, because $500 seemed like a lot of money. She quickly discovered that she was wrong on both counts.

The staff of Poland Union consisted of only three people: Ida, the school president, and Ida's assistant. In her first year, Ida taught classes in Greek, Latin, French, and German, as well as geology, botany, geometry, trigonometry, and extension classes for district schoolteachers throughout Ohio.

The extension classes were refresher courses on grammar and arithmetic. Most of the students in these classes were much older than Ida and had been teaching for years. Most had taken both courses several times, and inexperienced Ida struggled to teach these teachers who seemed to know all the right answers.

Finally, Ida realized why her teacher-students were so skilled—they used the same books and the same examples every year. They did not "know" the rules of grammar and arithmetic—they had memorized the answers. Ida developed new sentences and new math problems. Her students were outraged that her examples were not in their books. It was with great satisfaction that she told them that memorizing the answers was not nearly as important as understanding how to solve the problems.

In the two years she served as preceptress, this was Ida's only major conquest. The workload she carried would have staggered a less determined woman. At the same time, Ida found living on $500 a year impossible. To pay rent and buy food, she borrowed money from her father, much to her embarrassment. In 1882, she and the school president came to a mutual agreement: Ida was leaving. By the summer of that year, Ida was back in her tower room of the Tarbell's Titusville home peering into her microscope once again.

During the late 1800s, the Chautauqua Literary and Scientific Circle grew from a summer camp for training Sunday school teachers in western New York to a cultural, educational, and religious movement with a national following. Many of the program's supporters lived in rural areas, where the arrival of the Chautauqua tent show was the highlight of the year. These visitors enjoyed lectures, Shakespearean plays, Metropolitan opera concerts, or Broadway shows in a Chautauqua tent. The program also offered the first correspondence school degrees in the United States.

About six months after Ida returned from Poland, Ohio, Dr. Theodore Flood visited the Tarbells. Flood served as both a traveling minister and editor of the *Chautauquan* magazine. Many people who visited the Chautauqua tents during the summer subscribed to the magazine during the winter months. The magazine featured general interest articles, lessons, sermons, and discussions of Biblical material.

Because they had no access to dictionaries or libraries, many subscribers found the magazine too difficult to understand. Dr. Flood decided to help these readers by providing notes for the material presented each month. In Ida Tarbell, Flood found the ideal person to write those notes. Ida was well-educated, well-read, and familiar with the Chautauqua Circle, as her family had often attended summer lectures. Flood hired Ida as an assistant, his first editorial employee at the magazine.

Once again, Ida was employed, although the job was at first temporary. She moved thirty miles away to Meadville, the home of both Allegheny College and the *Chautauquan* publishing office. Ida knew nothing about printing or editing. However, she did bring to the job her intellect, her curiosity, and the attention to details she had developed studying science. She claimed, "A woman is a natural executive: that has been her business through the ages. Intuitively, she picks up, sets to rights, establishes order."

Ida threw herself into her new job. She spent hours writing notes to each article, always worried that she might omit something or make an error. When her regular work was done, she found other things to do in the publisher's office: proofreading copy, reviewing dummies, and checking on the accuracy of both ads and articles. She answered letters to the editor, mostly because Dr. Flood's responses were stiff and formal, while hers were more natural.

The head pressman, Adrian McCoy, admired Ida's dedication. He took it upon himself to train Ida in the language of the print shop. She learned that "dummies" were mock-ups of the final layout of the magazine. "Copy" was the text of an article, and "art" referred to all the illustrations and photography. In those days, type was set by hand and a good typesetter could set a line of type in about a minute, selecting each letter separately and spacing the letters and the line of type with a blank of lead, called "leading."

During Ida's time at the *Chautauquan*, the staff grew to include a small army of women. Much of the editorial content leaned toward women's issues of the day: voting, temperance, equal pay for equal work, and women's occupations. Guest writers such as Mary Livermore and Frances Willard provided articles promoting their points of view about drinking alcohol and women in the workplace.

It was not always clear which side of an issue the editorial staff supported. One month, they featured an article in favor of women staying home and being mothers. The next month's main article promoted women going out to work. The January 1884 issue of the magazine provided a comprehensive list of possible jobs women could do. Besides the standard teaching and nursing careers, photography, dry-goods sales, bookselling, dress or hat making, beekeeping, and poultry-raising were listed. Not one of these jobs required any education.

In 1887, Ida read an article that claimed only about

300 women had ever received United States patents for inventions. She knew this could not be true. Immediately, Ida headed to Washington, D.C., and had a meeting with the head of the U. S. Patent Office, R.C. McGill. On his own, McGill had already compiled a list of roughly 2,000 female patent holders. "Women As Inventors," by Ida Tarbell, was published in the March 1887 issue of the *Chautauquan.* In the article, Tarbell wrote, "Three things worth knowing and believing: that women have invented a large number of useful articles; that these patents are not confined to 'clothes and kitchen' devices as the skeptical masculine mind avers; that invention is a field in which woman has large possibilities."

Ida's "temporary" position at the *Chautauquan* turned into a seven-year job, which included the duties of associate editor, writer, and managing editor. She shared a house near the office with five women, all of whom worked on the magazine staff. Ida's long-term association with social reformers piqued her interest in voting, equal pay for equal work, temperance, and personal freedom. She still did not always agree with women's rights activists, but she did become interested in specific women and their efforts.

In particular, Madame Jeanne Manon Roland and Madame Germaine de Staël, two notable French women, drew Tarbell's attention. She wrote short articles about both women for the magazine but was determined to learn more about them. To do so, she felt she must go to Paris. There she would be able to do serious research. In

1889, Ida informed Dr. Flood that she was leaving. He was astounded. He asked how she would support herself in Europe. She replied that she would write. "You're not a writer," he said. "You'll starve."

Ida considered his words carefully. She knew she was not a writer in the sense that Mark Twain or Charles Dickens were writers. However, she was a methodical researcher, knew publishing, and was determined to succeed.

Ida returned to Titusville and prepared for her next adventure. She had translated French articles into English at the *Chautauquan*, but she worried that reading a language was quite different from speaking it. She arranged with Séraphin Claude, a local dyer and native French speaker, to learn how to speak the language properly. Three times a week she met with Claude and practiced French, speaking the phrases of daily life. Ida set her sights on Paris and never turned back.

Chapter Three

Paris on a Shoestring

Paris enchanted Ida and her three friends who joined her. The city during the "Gay Nineties" was alive with music and dancing, art and literature. It was the historic home of Louis Pasteur, Emile Zola, and Alexandre Dumas. Paris boasted a new tourist attraction: the Eiffel Tour, which was erected in 1889 for an international exhibit. Sidewalk cafes served coffee and croissants. The Moulin Rouge, with its red-lighted windmill, offered the can-can, a dance that scandalized some and thrilled many.

Paris was exhilarating—and expensive. After only a few days in a hotel, Ida suggested the young women look for an apartment. Ida's roommates—Jo Henderson and Mary Henry, co-workers from the *Chautauquan,* and Annie Towle—agreed, and Ida set out to find the most economical and practical rooms. She found the ideal location at 5 Rue du Sommerard, owned by Madame Bonnet. The four women piled into a tiny apartment that consisted of two small bedrooms, a living room, and a small kitchenette with a sink.

With limited money, the women often found themselves eating chicken or beef broth for lunch. They bought only as much food as they could eat in one meal, much as other Parisians did. Early each morning, Ida would run out to the local bakery to buy rolls and coffee for the group. Tarbell said, ". . . we leaned how to order at the cheap and orderly little restaurants of the [Latin] Quarter so as to get a sufficient meal of really excellent food for about a franc." In 1891, a franc was worth roughly twenty cents in U.S. money.

When friends came to visit, they were treated to a cup of tea. The ladies' entertainment budget was limited to a mere twelve cents per week. Of course, twelve cents bought much more in 1890s than it does today. Horse-drawn bus tours of Paris cost a penny per person. Tea for five or six, several times a week, fell well within the budgeted twelve cents.

Ida, at age thirty-four, had arrived in Paris with only about $150. She knew she would spend her money quickly, and she had a plan to provide much needed income. Before leaving for Paris, Ida had contacted several journals, hoping to interest the editors in articles on everyday French life from the viewpoint of an American living in Paris.

In the late 1800s, magazines and journals were the main media that brought news and literature to the public. There were no radios, movies, or television news broadcasts. Many writers presented their novels as segments in serial form. This includes such well-known authors as Sir Arthur Conan Doyle, O. Henry, and Mark Twain. Every major city had at least one newspaper. Many papers published both morning and evening editions to keep readers current with the news.

Ida hoped to interest some of these papers and magazines in her articles. The problem was, she needed to write the articles first and send them, hoping editors would buy her work. There was no guarantee that an article would be published or that she would be paid.

Almost immediately, Ida observed, noted, and wrote about what she saw: beggars, people at soup kitchens, and safety in the city. She volunteered at the soup kitchen on Faubourg Saint Antoine as part of her research. Her hard work paid off in November 1891 when Ida received her first payment for an article sent to the *Cincinnati Times-Star*—six dollars. It was enough money to buy food and a pair of much-needed shoes.

Soon, Ida's work regularly appeared in three newspapers: the *Pittsburgh Dispatch,* the *Cincinnati Times-Star,* and the *Chicago Tribune.* Ida began receiving regular checks, along with letters praising her work. In December 1891, Ida got a letter from yet another publisher, *Scribner's Magazine.* To her amazement, *Scribner's* bought a fictional story Ida had written called "France Adorée." The best news of all was the payment: a whopping $100 fee.

Her story vividly pictured everyday life in France. Here, she describes a Parisian woman leaving a bakery:

She wore a straight black skirt. Heavy shoes were on her feet. About her shoulders was drawn a knit shawl, the ends of which were knotted at her waist. Her head was bare, showing a mass of glossy black hair braided and coiled at the back. On her left arm the woman carried a square willow basket, in which one could see a bunch of the little red radishes with which, in their season, all Paris gives relish to their meals, and beside them a plump head of white cauliflower. In her right hand was a stick of bread at least three feet in length.

Paris was the center of the art world, and the four women regularly attended art shows held throughout the city. The Impressionist Movement in art that lasted roughly from 1870-1910 had begun in France. Impressionist artists chose everyday life as their primary subject. Ida and her friends found themselves walking through the same Paris shown in paintings by Degas, Monet, Manet, and Van Gogh. Ida described the French artists' techniques of using color: "The blues and greens fairly *howl* they are so bright and intense."

The publication of "France Adorée" made Ida a star among the Americans in Paris. Now, people became interested in the biography she was writing on Madame Manon Roland. Madame Roland lived during the French Revolution and was considered the driving force behind the Girondist political group. Members of the Girondists were from the educated middle class. They advocated war and a constitutional government. Roland

Tarbell's research on Madame Roland would eventually become the basis for a biography.
(Library of Congress)

attracted the interest of many politicians of her time through the many letters and essays she wrote. She favored the establishment of a republic in France, although her ideas of a democratic system were not very realistic. In 1792, Roland's husband became France's minister of the interior. While in office, Monsieur Roland carried out several acts that angered Paris citizens. Many felt his actions were spurred on by his wife's ideas. Madame Roland was arrested in May 1793 and sentenced to death. Just before her execution, she cried, "Liberty, what crimes are committed in thy name!"

Soon, a year in Paris came to an end, and Jo, Mary, and Annie returned to the U.S. Alone in Paris, Ida continued pursuing her education and researching Madame Roland. The promise of payments from various publishers kept Ida afloat, although the money was irritatingly slow to arrive.

Throughout her stay, Ida suffered twinges of homesickness. She wrote lengthy letters home and urged her mother to write at least once a week. She wanted to hear about everything: the family, Titusville, neighbors, church, and even which flowers were blooming in the garden.

In June 1892, Ida read with horror an account of a disaster in Titusville, her home town. According to the newspaper article, the city had been destroyed by a combination of flood and fire. Only the railroad station and an iron works remained standing. Ida was stunned. She imagined that her family was among the 150 people who had drowned or burned to death.

The worst part of the situation was Ida's inability to get definite news about her family. There were no phone lines into Titusville and no way to communicate with anyone there. Ida spent a restless, worry-filled night. The following morning, Ida's landlady knocked on the door with a cablegram. The message was only one word, but it was what Ida hoped to read: "Safe!"

A few weeks after the Titusville incident, a visitor arrived, anxious to speak with Ida. It was the editor Samuel Sidney McClure. Ida later described McClure as, "A slender figure, S.S. McClure, a shock of tumbled sandy hair, blue eyes which glowed and sparkled. He was close to my own age, a vibrant, eager, indomitable personality that electrified even the experienced and the cynical. His utter simplicity, outrightness, his enthusiasm and confidence captivated me."

They talked together for hours about McClure's plans to start a magazine that would promote social and political changes through investigative journalism. He had read some of Ida's articles and believed her to be the kind of editor he wanted for his new magazine. Their conversation ran so long that McClure missed his chance to go to the bank, and he ended their visit by borrowing $40 from Ida to pay for his train ticket. Ida had planned to use the money for a vacation, yet she gave it to McClure expecting to never see it again. She was wrong. Shortly after the visit, a check arrived from McClure's London office to repay his debt.

As tempting as McClure's offer was, Ida wanted to stay in Paris and finish her biography of Madame Roland. She contacted McClure and arranged to work as a freelance journalist in Paris. Better than the occasional check, Ida now had a string of writing assignments for McClure's magazine. The assignments meant regular work for regular money, something Ida had not enjoyed since arriving in Paris. Ida began by producing a number of articles about women intellectuals and writers in Paris. McClure also asked her to write about French and English scientists, their experiments and discoveries.

Among her first subjects was the renowned scientist Louis Pasteur. She interviewed Pasteur and his wife in their apartment over the Pasteur Institute. By this time, Pasteur was old, and he was paralyzed on his left side. Yet, he remained spirited and absorbed by everything around him.

The Pasteurs gave an easy interview. They were open, honest, and well-spoken. When Ida asked about family pictures, they opened their family albums and reviewed their lives with her. The Pasteur article was printed in September 1893, and Pasteur was delighted with it.

The promise of money from *McClure's* and *Scribner's*, although it was sometimes late in arriving, gave Ida the freedom to plunge deeply into her research

Publisher S.S. McClure was known for his tremendous energy and creativity.
(Library of Congress)

about Madame Roland. Friends in Paris introduced her to Léon Marillier, the great-great-grandson of Roland. This was the connection Tarbell had hoped for. Marillier provided access to Roland's letters, essays, and family papers. Better than that, Tarbell visited the Roland country estate, *Le Clos*, near Theizé. For Ida, the experience was like stepping back in time.

A red tile roof topped the classic white walls of *Le Clos*. Corner towers framed the estate house. The interior of the home had remained relatively unchanged during the century it was owned by the Roland family. The kitchen was large and dark, with a stone floor and a massive fireplace that had been used for cooking in earlier days.

Ida's suite was spare, consisting of a bedroom, a bathroom, and a study or sitting room. The walls and floor were bare, yet Ida hardly noticed because her study was filled with books—rare sets of Voltaire, Rousseau, and Diderot shared shelf space with scientific journals and histories. For Ida, this was heaven.

This personal view of Manon Roland was a mixed blessing. Ida had begun her work believing that Roland was an example of near-perfect womanhood and that her death was one of the great tragedies of the French Revolution. She ended up understanding that Manon Roland was just a woman with her own ambitions, weaknesses, and disappointments, much like every other woman in the world. Ida felt disappointed and disillusioned.

With the work on Roland done, it was time for Ida to

head home. She would join the staff of *McClure's* with a salary of $3,000 a year, which after years of scrimping, sounded like a fortune. Ida Tarbell first planned to take a lengthy vacation with her family in Titusville, and then she would move to New York City.

Chapter Four

Biographer

Ida returned home in 1894 to spend time with her family. Her father and mother still lived in the large Main Street house in Titusville. Brother Will had married, and he and his wife, Ella, had two daughters. Like Franklin, Will was an independent oilman. Ida's sister, Sarah, now a painter, lived at home with her parents. Like Ida, Sarah never married.

Ida had been dreadfully homesick during her stay in Paris, and she intended to pass several months at home before taking up her new job. However, S.S. McClure had other plans for her.

In June 1894, McClure wrote to Ida, asking her to meet with him in New York City. He needed her to start work immediately on a biography of Napoleon Bonaparte. The research would be based on material from Gardiner Green Hubbard's extensive Washington, D.C.-based collection of books and memoirs pertaining to Bonaparte, as well as letters and other information

Ida found at the U.S. State Department and in the capital's libraries. Hubbard was a dedicated collector of Bonaparte memorabilia, as well as being the father-in-law of Alexander Graham Bell. According to McClure, Ida would live at Twin Oaks, home of the Hubbards, in Washington, D.C. On top of Ida's forty dollar a week salary, this sounded like a good offer.

While Ida's salary would be very little money today, it was a huge sum in 1884. A family could easily eat for a week on ten dollars. Dinner in a restaurant—pork chops and gravy, mashed potatoes, and green beans—cost between forty cents and one dollar. Female factory workers, maids, cooks, and hatmakers rarely earned more than five dollars per week.

Once the biography was complete, a chapter would be printed each month in *McClure's*. This was Ida's second attempt at a long piece. Her first, the biography of Manon Roland, had taken several years to research and write. That leisurely pace did not meet with McClure's plans. He demanded that Napoleon must be finished in two months.

To Ida's surprise, there was more than enough information on Napoleon available in Washington, D.C. She scoured sources in the Library of Congress and the U.S. State Department. After trips to the city and hours spent in the Twin Oaks library, Ida often worked late into the night in her room.

Tarbell needed to learn as much as possible about Napoleon Bonaparte in the little time she had to do the research and writing. She already knew that he had been a French military leader who later became France's emperor. She discovered that Bonaparte entered government service as a young man. After helping to overthrow the government in 1799, Napoleon became the new leader of the French Republic.

Her biography vividly described the events that led to Napoleon being declared emperor of France. She detailed how his armies overran the neighboring countries of Belgium and Spain. In another installment, she explained that although considered a talented military strategist, Napoleon made a crucial error when he directed his army to invade Russia. Caught in the frigid Russian winter, Napoleon could do nothing but retreat.

Still another article told about the emperor being banished and sent into exile on the island of Elba. In 1815, Napoleon escaped from the island and was met by a welcoming army. Readers learned how Bonaparte again assumed the role of emperor and took the French to war. Tarbell recounted the Battle of Waterloo, where the British under Wellington defeated Napoleon's army. Her final installment told how Napoleon was exiled to St. Helena, where he remained under guard until his death in 1821.

The first installment of Napoleon's biography appeared six weeks after Ida started work. The series was a hit. Its success was the stuff *McClure's* magazine needed. The journal's circulation more than doubled after the first installment. When the last chapter finally printed, more than 100,000 copies were sold. Tarbell's quickly written "biography on the gallop," as she called it, was directly responsible for quadrupling *McClure's* readership.

As soon as Ida Tarbell finished the Napoleon series, McClure assigned her to write another biography, this one of Abraham Lincoln. The year was 1895, and Lincoln had been dead for thirty years. Ida, however, was not very interested in the assignment. She would rather continue writing about France, the country she loved so much, and its Revolution. One day, she even hoped to return to Paris.

McClure had researched each popular magazine thoroughly. Although many book-length biographies had been published about the famous president, no magazine had ever printed a series about Lincoln. McClure was an avid fan of Lincoln and considered him "the most vital factor in our life since the Civil War."

Despite the many Lincoln biographies, McClure was positive there was still plenty of information to be uncovered. That became Ida's job: to ferret out interesting stories, memories, letters, papers, and events that would interest *McClure's* readers.

Ida decided to direct her research on the people that had known Lincoln before his political fortune. Ida went to Kentucky, where Lincoln was born. She traveled by train, staying in small, often uncomfortable hotels. At one point, McClure became concerned about her health and asked whether she had sufficient bed socks to keep her warm.

As Tarbell followed Lincoln through his childhood,

young adulthood, early marriage, and to the White House, she slowly warmed to her subject. Along the way she met many people who had known the president, including Nicolay and Hay who had written one of the published Lincoln biographies. John Nicolay, once Lincoln's secretary, resented Ida's interest in Lincoln. He would do nothing to help her. However, that was not the general attitude of most people Ida met.

By the summer of 1896, Ida Tarbell could no longer cope with the rugged pace of traveling, interviewing, and writing. She was on the verge of a physical collapse. To regain her health, she checked into a sanitarium near Rochester, New York.

Clifton Springs Sanitarium was brand new when Ida arrived. Her recovery plan was based on rest, peace, attending religious services, and taking the water cure. Modern medicine at the turn of the century believed in the value of complete bed rest. In fact, Ida's doctors made her stay in bed all but two hours a day.

After a long period of constant work, doing nothing suited Ida. She enjoyed the opportunity to loll in bed. She often had a card on her door prohibiting visitors, which was surprisingly satisfying. Over the next thirty years, Ida retired to Clifton Springs yearly for rest and relaxation.

After recuperating at the sanitarium, Ida was ready to return to work on her Lincoln biography. Through Emily Lyons of Chicago, Ida was fortunate enough to meet Robert Lincoln, Abraham's son. Ida described the experience as an unbelievable thrill, although she said

Robert Lincoln assisted Tarbell in her research on his father.
(Library of Congress)

Robert Lincoln offered Tarbell a photograph of his father as a young man to illustrate the cover of *McClure's*. *(Library of Congress)*

Robert was nothing like his father. "He was all Todd [his mother's family], a big plump man perhaps fifty years old, perfectly groomed, with that freshness which makes men of his type look as if they were just out of the barber's chair . . . Robert Lincoln had had enough to crush him, but he was not crushed." Over tea, the two discussed Ida's project.

Robert Lincoln offered Ida a photograph that he thought was probably the earliest portrait of Lincoln ever made. To Ida's knowledge, no one knew this Lincoln. Later portraits showed a sad, homely man with the weight of the Civil War on his shoulders, but Robert's picture was of a young, good-looking, optimistic Lincoln. It was the perfect cover shot for *McClure's* next issue.

Ida collected many letters, pictures, and newspaper articles, which she compiled into a series called "The Life of Abraham Lincoln." The series did exactly what McClure had hoped—it boosted the magazine's circulation to over 250,000 copies.

For years, Tarbell met people who offered new or different memories about Lincoln. Previously unpublished letters and speeches came to Ida, to the extent that by 1899, she had a collection of more than 300 unpublished pieces. Her work on Lincoln took four years. During that time, she wrote articles, traveled to small towns, and talked with hundreds of people. Yet, once the work was complete, Ida felt there was still more to say. Between 1895 and 1915, she wrote five biographies about Lincoln, including *He Knew Lincoln* and *In the Footsteps of the Lincolns.* Although Ida enjoyed discovering the details of people's lives, her most enduring work was not her biographies. Her greatest acclaim would come from her next project for *McClure's.*

Chapter Five

Rockefeller and Standard Oil

The turn of the century found the staff of *McClure's* considering their next major assignments from a slightly jaded view. At that time, McClure himself was away, taking a rest cure in Switzerland. John Phillips was editor, Viola Roseboro served as "head reader," and the writing staff included Tarbell, Ray Stannard Baker, and Lincoln Steffens, among others.

Roseboro, Baker, and Steffens became close allies of Ida Tarbell, both in business and socially. Roseboro, according to Tarbell, was the "only born reader" Ida had ever met. Viola loved good writing and gave many unpublished, talented writers, such as Willa Cather, her support. Baker joined the staff after *McClure's* published a series of articles based on the memories of his uncle, a Civil War colonel and one of the men who captured John Wilkes Booth after Lincoln's assassination. It was Lincoln Steffens, however, that Ida considered the best of all journalists. She described him as young and self-confident—a professional who brought a new approach to journalism.

And, so it was, that in 1901, the group discussed "what to do next." It was agreed that they should look into the growth of business and the way millionaires made their money. By the end of the 1800s, a trend was occurring whereby many individual businesses in the United States had merged to form large corporations. These corporations, like in the case of Standard Oil, often took over many facets of an industry, such as drilling, refining, and selling oil, to become more efficient and profitable. Because federal law denied corporations the right to operate in more than one state, they also formed "trusts," a logistic loophole whereby a corporation would choose a board of trustees to supervise each segment of the corporation across state lines.

While this seemed to be simply the natural evolution of business, some of these corporations became so powerful that they wiped out competitors, controlled pricing, and even influenced federal laws. By the early 1900s, corporate giant General Electric commanded the manufacture and sale of electrical appliances. U.S. Steel Corporation, led by Andrew Carnegie, was the main player in the steel industry. American Telephone and Telegraph (AT&T) held a tight rein on communications. Standard Oil dominated the oil industry.

In many cases, trusts provided consumers with good quality products inexpensively. The problem with these giants was that they attempted to wipe out their competition by using unfair business practices. Such was the case with Frank and Will Tarbell and Ida's many neighbors in Titusville. The first antitrust law in the United States was the Sherman Anti-Trust Act of 1890. This act became the weapon which Presidents Theodore Roosevelt and William H. Taft used to break up the most powerful trusts, but it was nothing compared to the sting Rockefeller would feel from Ida Tarbell's pen.

Ida had grown up literally breathing, eating, and sleeping oil. Her father's finances quivered as the oil industry rose and fell. She had lived in the Oil Region in 1872 when Rockefeller had begun to buy out claims and refineries and the SIC had attempted to control shipping prices. Ida had personal memories of derricks, gushers, and puddles of black gold on the ground. She knew independent oilmen whose vast wealth was but a momentary fling before "big oil," in the shape of the Standard Oil Company, rose up like a dragon to destroy them.

Through her early adulthood, Ida learned about the actions of a few oil tycoons—John D. Rockefeller, in particular—through letters from her brother Will. William Tarbell was the financial manager and one of the founders of the Pure Oil Company, an independent oil business headquartered in Philadelphia. Will's bias against Rockefeller influenced Ida's viewpoint, although she liked to think of herself as impartial.

When the first oil wells were drilled in 1859, Rockefeller had recognized an opportunity. In 1873, he opened a petroleum refinery in Ohio. Within seven years, Rockefeller's company, Standard Oil Company,

Ida Tarbell focused her attack on big business on oil magnate John D. Rockefeller.
(Courtesy of the Rockefeller Archive Center)

was on its way to becoming an industrial giant. His rise to the top had meant stepping on plenty of toes. It is doubtful that he remembered the curious Ida Tarbell, a child whose family's well-being had been threatened by Rockefeller's business tactics. However, Ida remembered Rockefeller and the effect his actions had on her father and his friends.

By 1882, Standard Oil controlled ninety-five percent of all oil refining in the United States. Rockefeller also controlled shipping of crude petroleum and sale of refined oil, gas, and kerosene. Rockefeller, as the head of Standard Oil, became one of the wealthiest and most powerful men in the United States.

In September 1901, Ida set sail to Europe. She met with S.S. McClure to discuss her proposed series, "The History of the Standard Oil Company." In the beginning, the series would have three installments. Of course, McClure never committed himself so precisely that he could not expand a good thing. His goal was to sell magazines, and Tarbell's writing had several times increased circulation.

Back in New York, Ida began researching her subject. She had heard about a small pamphlet that had been compiled in 1873, entitled *The Rise and Fall of the South Improvement Company,* but she was having a hard time finding a copy. It seemed as though every copy had been destroyed, or, at least, disappeared. Ida tried in vain to locate a copy in the Titusville archives, in the private libraries of friends, or in the business libraries of independent oil companies. Having no luck, she tried her "last chance," and located a copy at the New York Public Library.

The contents of this pamphlet were important. Ida had guessed that Rockefeller had used the threat of SIC to force small companies to sell out to Standard Oil in 1872. Testimony in the pamphlet connected the SIC directly to John D. Rockefeller. This was the starting point of Ida's excavation into the workings of the United States' largest corporation.

Undertaking a project such as the investigation of the Standard Oil Company was too huge for even a workhorse like Ida. If she were to continue probing into the facts, Ida needed an assistant. She contacted several editors in Cleveland—the home base of Standard Oil—and asked them to recommend hardworking men who could keep their work secret. Three men were selected, and Ida asked each to find some pictures of the men who ran Standard Oil. While two of the three produced disappointing results, John McAlpin Siddall offered the level of interest, enthusiasm, and curiosity Ida needed. She immediately hired him for the job.

John Siddall, a young man in his late twenties, was round, short, and energetic. He had an automatic link to Tarbell because he worked at the *Chautauquan.* He and Ida shared many similar traits: attention to details, willingness to follow every lead to its conclusion, and a creative approach to each project. Through Siddall, Ida gained access to Mr. Frank Rockefeller, John D.'s brother, who provided pictures and information about John as a young man. Siddall also had connections to the photo archives of the *Cleveland Plain Dealer.* Siddall became Tarbell's researcher, lifelong friend, and colleague.

Ida and John Siddall were well into their investigations when writer Mark Twain showed up at the McClure offices. Twain's work had appeared in *McClure's* and he and Ida were acquaintances. He asked if Ida would be interested in meeting with Henry Rogers, a friend of Twain's who was also one of John Rockefeller's partners in the Standard Oil Company.

Whatever Ida expected, it was not meeting a charming, gracious man with excellent manners. Henry Rogers was a former independent oilman who once challenged Rockefeller by leading refiners against him and the South Improvement Company. He remembered Franklin Tarbell and Ida as a young girl. The journalist and the businessman met at his New York City home in January 1902. Ida described him as "a striking figure, by all odds the handsomest and most distinguished figure in Wall Street . . . There was a trace of the early oil adventure in his bearing in spite of his air of authority, his excellent grooming, his manner of the quick-witted naturally adaptable man who has seen much of people."

At their first meeting, Ida and Henry agreed that she would continue to use him as a sounding board for case histories she uncovered in her research. He would back up Standard Oil's position in each case with original documents, letters, or statistics.

Although the two met often, Ida could never consider Rogers an ally. For one thing, their meetings were bizarre. She arrived at the Standard Oil offices on Broad-

Writer Mark Twain was close friends with Standard Oil executive Henry Rogers.
(Library of Congress)

way. There, she was met by a different young man every time, then sprinted through hallways and side rooms to meet with Rogers. Her exit was equally strange. In the many times Tarbell met with Rogers at Standard Oil, she never saw any of the same people twice—except Rogers himself.

Tarbell met with Henry Rogers while researching her *History of Standard Oil. (Library of Congress)*

When the first installment of the Standard Oil series was printed, Ida expected Rogers to refuse her any further meetings. However, that was not so. The facts presented were accurate; their views of the importance of the facts differed. Ida's early bias against all things Rockefeller led her to find the faults and failings of Standard Oil while Rogers saw the good resulting from each step the company had taken. The series voiced both the facts and Ida's opinion of fair business:

> The truth is, blackmail and every other business vice is the natural result of the peculiar business practices of the Standard. If business is to be treated as warfare and not as a peaceful pursuit, as they have persisted in treating it, they cannot expect the men they are fighting to lie down and die without a struggle. If they get special privileges, they must expect their

competitors to struggle to get them. If they will find it more profitable to buy out a refinery than to let it live, they must expect the owner to get an extortionate price if he can. And when they complain of these practices and call them blackmail, they show thin sporting blood. They must not expect to monopolize hard dealings, if they do oil.

While Ida was at work on the Standard Oil history, tragedy struck the Tarbell family. Franklin Tarbell died in 1905, after a long illness. Ida felt a tremendous sense of loss. She had always loved her father dearly and described him as "modest, humorous, hard-working, friendly, faithful in what he conceived to be the right." To overcome her grief, Ida threw herself deeper into her work.

There had been many stories that claimed John D. Rockefeller rose to the top by unfair, underhanded business practices. Rumors flew about forcing owners to sell up, controlling oil prices, destroying shipments, and getting massive rebates from railroad shipping costs. Ida was determined to uncover the truth of every accusation.

For three decades, independents claimed that their oil shipments were tampered with. The independents didn't know exactly how it happened, but they were sure there was a problem. Their shipments often arrived late, and sometimes not at all.

During her investigation, documents came to Tarbell from an employee of the Standard Oil Company about a plot between Rockefeller and the railroads. A young man had been hired to work at Standard Oil. One of his jobs was to burn old papers. As he was doing so, he came across a name that he recognized, that of a man who had been his Sunday school teacher and who was one of Standard Oil's competitors.

The young man began to see his former teacher's name frequently. Every paper was a railroad shipping order, stating the destination, day and amount of the oil shipment. On one notice, there was a comment, "Stop that shipment—get that trade." The young man collected each of the documents and turned them over to his friend. In turn, that friend handed Ida Tarbell the evidence she had been looking for—Standard Oil had engaged in acts of sabotage. Agents of Standard Oil tipped over tankers and drained shipments by independent oilmen, and did so based on information fed to them by the railroad companies themselves.

The best-known claim Tarbell laid at Rockefeller's feet was his treatment of Fred Backus' widow. According to Tarbell, Rockefeller bought out Mr. Backus' lubricating plant at a rock bottom price, effectively robbing the widow. According to Rockefeller, the claim was completely false. His version tells of Backus as a former employee who opened his own company and ran into trouble. Backus died of consumption, leaving behind a useless and valueless business, which Rockefeller bought four years after Backus' death. Although there was evidence available that Standard Oil had paid a more than fair price for what was small business, Tarbell decided to publish the version of the story that put Rockefeller in the worst light. She also failed to mention that the Widow Backus invested the money she received in Cleveland real estate and died a wealthy woman. Whether true or not, many readers believed Tarbell's version, and Rockefeller's reputation was blackened further.

In the midst of her research, Ida itched to meet Rockefeller face-to-face. However, Rockefeller refused any and all invitations to meet with the journalist. Siddall proposed that a viable alternative would be to observe Rockefeller at the church he attended regularly.

One Sunday, Ida and John Siddall headed off to a rally at Rockefeller's Baptist church. After they were seated, Rockefeller entered the church. According to Ida, "There was an awful age in his face—the oldest man I had ever seen, I thought, but what power! . . . His eyes were never quiet but darted from face to face, even peering around the job at the audience close to the wall." At the church rally, Rockefeller spoke to the congregation, and Ida was surprised by how clear and strong his voice was as compared to his physical appearance.

While she did not admire his business practices, Ida tried to be fair about Rockefeller's generosity. From his youth, Rockefeller had tithed—given ten percent—of his income to the church. As his wealth grew, so did the value of his contributions. Between 1886 and 1904, Rockefeller donated $35 million to various churches, colleges, and worthy causes.

Tarbell recognized that John Rockefeller had a brilliant business mind. She said, "With Mr. Rockefeller's genius for detail, there went a sense of the big and vital factors in the oil business and a daring in laying hold of them which was very like military genius. He saw strategic points like a Napoleon and he swooped on them with the suddenness of a Napoleon."

John D. Rockefeller never met Ida Tarbell, but he knew of her, and, to an extent, knew her personality. He believed that she displayed a false modesty about her success, which he said, "is simply covering up her wrath and her jealousy which were all the time present, but which she did not show all the time and which she thought she could bring out all the better by weaving this in a silken thread. She makes a pretense of fairness."

Rockefeller did not see himself as a titan beating the small business man to a pulp, but as a savior of the independent who struggled against huge odds in an industry where fortunes were made and lost in mere days. He felt it was wrong for Tarbell to call "it a crime that these men were delivered from their sinking ships. It was a great mercy and without precedent . . ."

The History of the Standard Oil Company was written in a strong, clear style. Instead of openly condemning Rockefeller and Standard Oil, Ida selected anecdotes and details that furthered her point of view, presenting them in an understated manner. This gave the work the appearance of objectivity, although it is clear she was never objective about Rockefeller and Stan-

Tarbell based her character sketch of John D. Rockefeller, in part, on her visit to his church. *(Library of Congress)*

dard Oil. She had watched too many men live in fear of the oil trust to distance herself from her feelings. Ultimately, her series on Standard Oil is a work of brilliant propaganda. However, Rockefeller (who had recently retired from Standard Oil) and the company's directors made a mistake when they did not react to counter the charges Ida made in the articles. The little girl of the oil patch, who had watched her father worry about the South Improvement scheme, finally got her revenge.

Although Ida Tarbell's father had warned her that Rockefeller would destroy *McClure's* if she wrote the series, the articles were so popular the magazine's circulation more than doubled to 375,000 issues. To keep the momentum going, McClure changed his original plan and asked for more chapters. In all, nineteen chapters were published, and by the end she had done more than any other person to turn public opinion against Standard Oil.

Tarbell and Siddall were anxious to hear what Rockefeller had to say about them. Siddall asked Hiram Brown, a long-time friend of Rockefeller, to ask the oilman's response to Tarbell's work. "At the mention of Tarbell's name, Rockefeller steadied himself with a long breath. 'I tell you, Hiram, things have changed since you and I were boys. The world is full of socialists and anarchists. Whenever a man succeeds remarkably in any particular line of business, they jump on him and cry him down.' "

As popular pressure grew, the government began investigating Standard Oil. In 1906, a lawsuit was filed against the company, claiming that it had violated the Sherman Anti-Trust Act. The government accused Standard Oil of unfair business practices, which led to the creation of a monopoly. Standard Oil was found guilty of the charges, but appealed the findings. In 1911, the U.S. Supreme Court upheld the lower court's decision. Standard Oil had to dissolve its gigantic corporation into thirty-eight smaller companies. Among those newly-formed companies are today's Exxon, Mobil, Chevron, and Amoco. Ironically, the break-up made Rockefeller a much wealthier man, because the value of the stock had been suppressed when it was part of the trust. It also allowed the companies, which were now smaller and more flexible, to better respond to the advent of the automobile which, of course, enlarged Rockefeller's fortune even more.

Besides the break-up of Standard Oil, Tarbell's work spurred the government to make new laws to control powerful corporations. These laws were the Hepburn Act of 1906, the Mann-Elkins Act of 1910, and the Clayton Act of 1914. The Hepburn Act stopped underhanded shipping negotiations between corporate giants and the railroads by controlling railroad freight rates. Mann-Elkins gave the Interstate Commerce Commission the power to oversee oil pipeline rates. The Clayton Act made unfair business practices illegal, particularly if those practices led to building a monopoly.

The series also changed Ida Tarbell's career. She became one of the best-known women in the United States. She also came to be called a "muckraker," a term which she did not always appreciate.

Chapter Six

Muckraker

The year 1906 brought changes to Ida Tarbell's life that she had not anticipated. In that one year she was labeled a "muckraker," bought a house, and left *McClure's.*

In the early 1900s, several journalists set out to prove that the pen truly was mightier than the sword. These magazine writers put politicians, corporations, and social practices under a microscope. They investigated every aspect of their subjects, then wrote articles exposing the subject's wrongdoings. Among these writers were Ida M. Tarbell, Lincoln Steffens, Upton Sinclair, Ray Stannard Baker, and David Graham Phillips.

One subject that caught the attention of these investigative journalists was the United States Senate. Repeated attacks on the Senate caused President Theodore Roosevelt to label these writers "muckrakers." The name came from John Bunyan's *Pilgrim's Progress* in which the Man with the Muckrake forever clears muck from the floor. He never looks up, only down at the filth. Roosevelt said, "The man who never does anything else, who never thinks or speaks or writes save of his feats with the muckrake, speedily becomes, not a help to society, not an incitement to good, but one of the most potent forces of evil."

In the beginning, the term annoyed Tarbell, because she did not feel her work was steeped in muck. Also, she noted that Roosevelt had obviously misunderstood Bunyan's Man with the Muckrake—a character who was raking in riches. Tarbell felt this better applied to Rockefeller than to her. Once she realized how much *McClure's* readers admired her efforts, however, she began to consider being a muckraker as a compliment.

Tarbell is often considered the first of the muckrakers because she began researching *The History of the Standard Oil Company* before Lincoln Steffens published his first exposé on political corruption in Minneapolis. However, Tarbell's first chapter about Standard Oil, Steffens' article, and a scathing investigation of labor unions by Ray Stannard Baker all appeared in the January 1903 issue of *McClure's Magazine.* A new era in journalism had begun.

Muckraking was the forerunner of investigative journalism. The writers chose from a wide range of topics—political corruption, illegal or unethical business practices, public health and safety, to name a few. Their goal was to bring about change by informing the public. Muckrakers were the first journalists who based their writing on the public's "right to know."

Journalists Lincoln Steffens (left) and Ray Stannard Baker (below) became famous along with Ida Tarbell for exposing corruption in American society.
(Library of Congress)

For some years, Ida had been longing for a home of her own. Titusville, still the home of her mother, her brother and his family, and her sister Sarah, was too far away to be considered home anymore. For Ida, who spent almost as much time on the road as she did in New York, there was no retreat from the bustle of the big city, no place to put up her feet and relax.

In Redding Ridge, a town in rural Connecticut, Ida bought a farm situated on forty acres of land, which she called Twin Oaks, like the Hubbard's home in Washington, D.C. She had planned to let the house and land take care of themselves, but that was not to be. Said Ida,

> Things happened: the roof leaked; the grass must be cut if I was to have a comfortable sward to sit on; water in the house was imperative. And what I had not reckoned with came from all the corners of my land: incessant calls—fields calling to be rid of underbrush and weeds and turned to their proper work; a garden spot calling for a chance to show what it could do; apple trees begging to be trimmed and sprayed. I had bought an abandoned farm, and it cried loud to go about its business.

The next thing Ida knew, she was arranging for the fields to be plowed and livestock to be bought. The neglected orchard was pruned. Chickens clucked in the barnyard, while Ida's strained finances stretched to support horses, a cow, and a pig. She even passed up buying a swanky dress in favor of buying manure to fertilize the garden.

The farm became both a refuge and the center of Ida's social life. She lived near Mark Twain and a host of other people from the New York publishing world. The rural life suited Ida well, and she often entertained friends from the city for a weekend.

At *McClure's*, Ida and John Phillips became more involved in running the magazine, while S.S. McClure became an absentee editor. McClure no longer wanted to deal in the day-to-day workings of the magazine, nor did he want to completely give up his control. At times, McClure supported Tarbell and Phillips, then turned around and overrode their orders. The strain of such a working relationship began to affect the staff. Slowly, Ida and John Phillips grew disillusioned with McClure's erratic attitudes.

In March 1906, Ida and John Phillips resigned from *McClure's*. They were followed by Ray Stannard Baker, Lincoln Steffens, and John Siddall. For Ida, it was the first time in twelve years that she was jobless.

Phillips was not a man to enjoy idleness. He and Ida purchased the *American Magazine* under management of the newly formed Phillips Publishing Company. Although she helped raise money for Phillips to buy out the *American Magazine,* Ida was not a member of the management team. Phillips was its president, Lincoln Steffens served as vice-president, and Boyden—a former *McClure's* editor—served as secretary. The magazine's goal was to speak out in favor of reform. Rather than direct a reader's attention to what was "wrong" in society, the *American Magazine* also tried to point out what was "right."

Tarbell bought a farm in the country to use as a retreat from her busy schedule in New York. *(Library of Congress)*

Almost immediately Ida began investigating her next major topic: tariffs. Most people in the 1900s believed that tariffs—duties on imported goods—were needed to protect American businesses. The greatest defenders of tariffs were those who received the benefits. Tariffs existed on beef and leather, cotton and wool, sugar, and metals such as tin and iron. Ida believed that these tariffs not only added to the profits of major companies, but also hurt the average person who bought food, clothing, and other goods at higher prices.

A tariff is a tax on imported goods. The goal behind a tariff is to protect a country's industries from competition from foreign companies. Tariffs can be set in one of three ways: by the volume or weight of product, by the dollar value of product, or a combination of both. Weight-based tariffs are placed on goods sold in quantity, like iron ore, sugar, or cotton. Value-based tariffs are placed on goods sold individually, such as cars or television sets. A combination tariff would be placed on products that are both value and volume driven, such as denim for jeans or silicon chips for computers. Few people understood the effects of tariffs on their jobs, their wages, and their purchasing power.

The *American Magazine* published the first installment of the tariff series in its second issue, December 1906. Tarbell's opening article addressed the history of tariffs in the United States, and the readers' reactions were ho-hum. For the most part, the public could not see how they were damaged by tariffs protecting American businesses. It was not until 1908, when Tarbell wrote

"Every Penny Counts" that the public realized the real cost of tariffs.

In that article, Ida Tarbell related a number of tariffs to everyday purchases by American consumers. She explained how much more shoes, clothes, food, and even thread cost because of tariffs. She showed how a few cents on each tariff-protected item added up to dollars out of the average American pocket. Suddenly, readers realized exactly how they were hurt by tariffs and cried for change.

One of Tarbell's most interesting tariff-based articles was "A Tariff-Made City," which attacked the government's protection of U.S. Steel. Tarbell claimed that Pittsburgh had benefited for over fifty years by protective tariffs. She explained that tariffs were supposedly designed to protect and advance the worker, yet she claimed those who reaped the benefits were the millionaires who grew richer off the labor of others.

Tarbell pointed out that steel mill workers endured twelve-hour days, seven days a week. Those workers did not even enjoy decent living conditions. She said, "For years the death rate from typhoid fever in Pittsburgh had been the highest of any city in the civilized world . . . There was no supply of pure drinking water . . . The conditions under which the children of the poor are brought up in Pittsburgh are such that babies die like flies."

Once again, the government was forced to take action because of Ida Tarbell's work. For years, private interest groups had donated money to members of the

U.S. Congress in return for their support of protective tariffs. Now, those same U.S. Senators and Representatives were being pressured by public outrage to get the tariff issue under control. In 1909, a battle ensued in Congress over the Payne Tariff Bill. In its original form, the bill removed tariffs on coal, iron, tanned hides, flax, and wood pulp. In the Senate, Rhode Island's Nelson Aldrich fought for compromise. By the time the bill was passed in Congress, it was called the Payne-Aldrich Tariff Act. The new law restored tariffs to most protected goods, to the dismay of an angry public.

Among Ida's early assignments was investigating how Chicago had handled public transportation. In 1908, she headed to Chicago and took up residence in Hull House, the creation of social reformer Jane Addams and Ellen Gates Starr.

Hull House provided housing, education, job training, and childcare for women and families in the Chicago slums. At Hull House, immigrant women learned to speak English, trained for a job, and developed homemaking skills. While they worked, their children were cared for at the shelter.

Addams was also a pacifist who actively worked for peace throughout the world. She served as chairperson of the Women's Peace Party and was president of the International Congress of Women. Jane Addams was honored with the Nobel Peace Prize in 1931. Her efforts for social change provided many women with an opportunity for financial and family security.

While at Hull House, Tarbell took part in a number of

In Chicago, Jane Addams helped poor women and their children at Hull House by providing them with shelter, food, day care and job training. *(Library of Congress)*

the group's programs. The transportation article was of little reader interest, but the opportunity to become friends with Jane Addams was invaluable.

On the whole, Tarbell admired Addams. Both women had investigated the model of Toynbee Hall, London, England, during the 1880s. Toynbee Hall was a settlement house for people who lived in London's slums. The program was begun to help people develop skills that would allow them to work, earn money, and support themselves. Tarbell wrote about the social experiment of Toynbee for the *Chautauquan,* while Addams took the Toynbee practices to Hull House. In 1908, there were few women in the United States who were as well-known or well-respected as Addams and Tarbell.

Years of muckraking against trusts and tariffs had given Ida Tarbell a view of how most Americans made their living. She knew that there was injustice and abuse in factories, just as she knew that there were enlightened, intelligent owners who tried to provide their workers with a good living.

Ida proposed that she study the positive side of business and industry. "Was it not the duty of those who were called muckrakers to rake up the good earth as well as the noxious?" The editors of the *American Magazine* agreed. From 1912 through 1916, Ida toured the U.S. visiting every type of factory imaginable, writing:

> The work took me from Maine to Alabama, from New York to Kansas. I found my material in all sorts of industries: iron and steel in and around Pittsburgh, Chicago, Duluth; mines in West Virginia, Illinois,

and Wisconsin; paper boxes and books and newspapers everywhere; candy in Philadelphia; beer and tanneries and woodwork in Wisconsin; shirts and collars and shoes in New York and Massachusetts.

Everywhere she met with mixed greetings. Many factory managers believed she was anti-business and wanted to avoid her. On the other hand, some of those same men had also read her biography of Lincoln, and they approved of some of her work. Mostly, even those with negative opinions allowed Ida access to the factory floor. She spent hours watching cloth being woven, buttons made, thread spooled. She saw fine china and everyday pots come off the line.

In most places, she not only investigated the workplace, but also the way workers and their families lived. During these years, she met two men whose enlightened ideas on labor impressed her: Thomas Lynch and Henry Ford.

Lynch was president of the Frick Coke Company. He had risen through the ranks, beginning as a miner. Lynch promoted the idea of "Safety First," believing that it was better to prevent mining accidents than to launch rescues. As president, Lynch wanted his employees to have decent living conditions. He provided solid mill houses with running water, located on land that could support a garden. In the early 1910s, this was a revolutionary idea. Further, he promoted gardening by offering prizes for the best kept plots.

Tarbell reported the success of Lynch's plan: "In 1914, when I was first there, out of 7,000 homes, 6,923 had gardens. And such gardens! It took three days for Mr. Lynch and two or three other distinguished gentlemen to decide the winners of the nine prizes given for the finest displays. They were estimating that the vegetables gardens yielded $143,000 worth of vegetables that year." Lynch had given his workers more than just housing, he had given them pride.

Henry Ford, founder of the Ford Motor Company, fascinated Ida Tarbell. He was easy-going, humorous, and a creative manager. Ford's plan, according to Ida, was to make not just products, but men. He began by offering a minimum wage of $5.00 per day—high pay for, he hoped, excellent work. Ford was not disappointed. He was able to build more cars, faster, better, and cheaper, so that the average worker in his plant could afford to buy the products Ford employees built.

Tarbell admired Ford's views on mass production, which she recorded in her autobiography:

> The trouble's been we didn't pay men enough. High wages pay. People do more work. We never thought we'd get back our five dollars a day; didn't think of it; just thought that something was wrong that so many people were out of work and hadn't anything saved up, and thought we ought to divide . . . Of course when you're building and trying new things all the time you've got to have money; but you get it if you make men. I don't know that our scheme is best. It will take five years to try it out, but we are doing the best we can and changing when we strike a snag.

Tarbell admired automobile manufacturer Henry Ford's business principles.
(Library of Congress)

Ida's interest in workers and working conditions continued for many years. In an undated article, possibly written in 1925, she wrote about a tragedy in Kentucky. The article, entitled "The Floyd Collinses of Our Mines," detailed the unfortunate death of young Floyd Collins, who was victim of a rock slide while exploring an underground cave near Cave City. Tarbell explained that everything humanly possible was done—at great cost—to save this one adventurer. Ida then compared the concern shown over this one man to the negligence the coal industry showed its miners:

> Every year over NINE HUNDRED bituminous coal miners are tombed in American mines as he [Collins] was. Falling earth, rocks, timber, coal, trap them. They die victims of industry—part of the price we pay for warmth and flying wheels . . . Nine hundred Floyd Collinses a year—nine thousand in ten years—and we treat the awful toll as a necessary incident to keeping the world running . . .

Tarbell made an accusation that neither mine owners nor legislators could deny. At the time there were many new techniques for making mining safer, yet they were not used by owners because they cost money. In the same article, she wondered why the government had not demanded safer conditions in mines, knowing that safety factors could save lives. In this issue, as in previous ones, Tarbell needled the consciences of men who put profit ahead of people.

Chapter Seven

The Business of Being a Woman

During her years of investigating the positive side of industry, Ida Tarbell also wrote a series for the *American Magazine* on women, examining their roles and their obligations in society. In the early 1900s, suffragettes marched in favor of women voting. Temperance leaders rallied thousands against the perils of "demon rum." Women fought for equal pay for equal work. Women challenged their traditional roles in every arena, including the home.

There were few women in high-paying professions: doctors, dentists, lawyers, and such. Women had political opinions, but few held political offices. Women worked in factories, but few owned or managed them. Working women were expected to enter "acceptable" fields: teaching, nursing, cooking, or serving as maids.

Considering how free and adventuresome Ida Tarbell's life had been to this point, people expected her to champion women in professions, women voting, birth control, and other feminist issues. But, if readers expected her to promote women and women's causes in her writing, they were sadly disappointed. She emphatically did not.

In fact, Ida Tarbell's views of women and their place in the world was inconsistent. At the *Chautauquan,* Ida worked mainly with women and wrote about women's issues. In "Women as Inventors," she plainly stated that women were in all ways suited to inventing new, practical devices. In another article written around that time, she suggested that there is no particular reason that women can not succeed in journalism. Tarbell said, "If one has proved herself capable, work can nearly always be obtained with ease. A successful journalist must progress in ideas, in information, in capacity for work; this fact makes the calling particularly desirable." She went on to give a list of the character traits needed for a woman to succeed, including the ability to follow directions, the willingness to take on any task, persistence, a crisp writing style, self-control, and accuracy.

Yet, although Tarbell herself refused to ever marry and have children, she said, "The central fact of the woman's life—nature's reason for her—is the child, his bearing and rearing. There is no escaping the divine order that her life must be built around this constraint, duty, or privilege . . ."

When investigating family life as part of her industry research, Tarbell noted, "I spent quite as much time looking at homes as at plants . . . I found even in the most barren and unattractive company districts women who had made attractive homes . . . The pride of the man who had a good housekeeper as a wife, a good cook, was great." Once again, Tarbell advanced the value of being a good housewife, a position she herself refused to conform to.

In February 1912, the *American Magazine* published Tarbell's "Making a Man of Herself." In this article, Ida declared that some complaints voiced by women were fair. She agreed that women should be allowed to have outside interests so that they would not be bored with life once their children were grown. She also stated that women, for the most part, lacked the ability to see and achieve real greatness. Tarbell's readers were furious.

Feminists criticized Tarbell's view of women's causes in a rally held in New York City. Other women's activists tried to convince Tarbell to help them with no success.

One of these women was Helen Keller. Keller was a remarkable woman who had overcome blindness and deafness to gain an education and speak on behalf of handicapped people throughout the world. Keller was an ardent suffragist, only half Tarbell's age. She was disappointed to learn that Tarbell was against women's suffrage, and declared that Ida was simply too old to appreciate the need to change.

In truth, Tarbell insisted she was neither in favor of women voting, nor against it. She did say, however,

> Feeling as I did, I could not fight for suffrage, although I did not fight against it . . . I believed that it would come because in the minds of most people

democracy is a piece of machinery, its motive power the ballot. The majority of advocates for women's suffrage saw regeneration, a new world through laws and systems . . . What I feared in women was that they would substitute the letter for the spirit, weaken the strategic place Nature and society had given them . . .

Margaret Sanger, founder of Planned Parenthood, contacted Ida and asked her to support a national conference in favor of birth control. Tarbell's response to Sanger's request was negative. She felt that this was an area for doctors, parents, and social workers to pursue. Since Ida was none of these, she had not given the matter much consideration and could not support it.

Tarbell compiled her essays about women into a book entitled *The Business of Being a Woman.* The book was as poorly received as the articles had been. Said Tarbell, "That title was like a red rag to many of my militant friends. The idea that woman had a business assigned by nature and society which was of more importance than public life disturbed them; even if it was so, they did not want it emphasized."

It would seem that Ida Tarbell had little time for outside interests, considering her extensive research and writing schedule, but she was extremely sociable. She filled her extra time with family, friends, and women's social clubs.

In 1908, after visiting Jane Addams in Chicago, Ida had stopped in Pennsylvania for a visit with her mother and sister, Sarah. She found her mother's health failing and immediately arranged for Esther Tarbell to be placed in a nursing home. Sarah returned to Connecticut with Ida, where she remained. Sarah eventually bought five acres of land from Ida and built her own cottage there.

Esther spent time with her daughters in Connecticut during the summer months of each year. Esther was never one to hold her opinion, even with her famous daughter. Esther supported women's suffrage, and openly criticized Ida's failure to support the cause.

Despite a heavy schedule, Ida Tarbell joined many clubs. Her memberships were extensive, although she did not always attend many meetings. However, she regularly supported and participated in three clubs: the Colony, the Cosmopolitan, and the Pen and Brush. It was in the Pen and Brush that Ida became most active. The group was a social club for women artists and writers. In 1913, Ida agreed to serve as the club's president. She held that position for a total of thirty years. While Ida happily attended meetings, invited friends for the weekend, and wrote continuously, changes were coming that Ida never anticipated. The winds of war were sweeping across Europe.

Chapter Eight

A World Gone Mad

In 1914, the Archduke Ferdinand, heir to the throne of Austria-Hungary, was assassinated in Sarajevo, the capital of Bosnia. This incident sparked a war between the Central Powers (primarily Germany, Austria-Hungary, and the Ottoman Empire) and the Allies (mainly Great Britain, France, Russia, and, eventually, the United States). Within weeks, major European powers chose sides and four years of conflict began. At that time, the United States government did not want to take sides in the war and tried to remain neutral.

Even though the U.S. was not fighting, World War I affected the lives of Americans. This was true for Ida Tarbell, who had hoped to spend her remaining productive years writing for the *American Magazine.*

In 1915, the *American* was sold to another publishing company. John Siddall, Ida's assistant during her years of writing about John D. Rockefeller and Standard Oil, was named editor. Ida recognized that her style of writing no longer fit into the editorial scheme of the *American.* She was, once again, out of work.

Ida's career took a strange, but natural, bend when she was approached to join the ranks of Chautauqua guest speakers by Louis Alber of the Coit Alber Lecture Bureau. The lecture bureau booked speakers for events, conventions, and, most particularly, the Chautauqua Science and Literary Circuit.

Ida considered the offer to become a speaker carefully. "I was free, and I might forget the situation in which I found myself by undertaking a new type of work . . . Mr. Alber wanted me to speak on these New Ideals in Business which I had been discussing in the magazine . . . At all events I signed up for a seven weeks' circuit, forty-nine days in forty-nine different places."

Speaking in public in 1915 was very different from speaking today. The tents were lighted much like a county fair. There were no television monitors, overhead projectors, or slide shows. There was no microphone with amplifiers that reached the farthest corners of the auditorium. A speaker had to present her material in a voice that carried to the last row of seats. Ida had never done much public speaking, and certainly not of the type that held Chautauqua audiences spellbound.

In her usual methodical style, she prepared by taking speech lessons with Frank Sargent of the American Academy of Dramatic Arts. She remembered:

He began by putting me on the simplest exercises but

> with severe instructions about keeping them up. I went about my apartment day and night shouting 'Ma, Me, Mi, Mo,' 'Ba, Be, Bi, Bo.' I learned that the voice must come from the diaphragm . . . Regularly every morning and every night, lying on my back with books on my stomach, I breathed deeply until I could lift four or five volumes.

The reality of speaking in forty-nine different places in as many days struck early. Ida's schedule was strict—rise, bathe, dress, travel, eat, speak, sleep. Ida had always considered herself a good traveler. After all, she had seen much of the eastern and mid-western United States researching her many articles. However, there was a difference between keeping to her own schedule and following the speaker's bureau schedule. Ida became obsessed about the comfort available at each hotel. "Are there bathrooms? If so, am I to get one?" she would ask.

In fact, the Chautauqua circuit was much like being part of a traveling circus. There were the headliners, the music, and the support staff. Each tent was decorated, lit, clean, and tidy. Ida's traveling group included bell ringers, trained dogs, and yodelers. There were singers and another speaker named Sydney Landon, a lawyer with extensive experience on the circuit. In all, it was a lively, active, and thoroughly professional group. Ida learned to live with the irregularities of train travel, strange hotels and beds, and eating on the run.

Ida finished her commitment, tired and pleased. If

nothing else, she had survived, and the money she earned would pay many outstanding bills. She signed up for additional tours over the next few years.

When World War I began in 1914, President Woodrow Wilson wanted the United States to remain neutral. Germany, however, continued to sink American ships. In February 1917, Wilson broke off diplomatic relations with Germany. That same day, the American steamship *Housatonic* was attacked and sunk by a German submarine. Over the next few weeks, several other American ships were sunk. In April, the United States declared war against Germany and the other Central Powers.

When the United States finally entered World War I, people from every profession was asked to support the war effort. Ida was speaking in Cleveland in April 1917, when she received a telegram from President Woodrow Wilson. She had met Wilson on several previous occasions and had dined with the president and Mrs. Wilson at a friend's home in Washington, D.C., the previous year. Now, the president was asking her to be part of the Women's Committee of the Council of National Defense.

The first meeting of the Women's Committee of the Council of National Defense was an event. The women were ready, but no place had been set for their meeting. They finally found a vacant room, then had to hunt for chairs so the committee members could sit down. Ida later wrote, "My first contribution to winning the War was looting chairs from adjacent offices. My success gave me hope that after all I might be at least an errand boy in the war machine."

The goal of the Women's Committee was to mobilize the nation's women in support of the war effort. The committee members represented the most powerful women's groups of the time: suffragists, temperance groups, social service clubs, and groups with historical leanings, such as the Colonial Dames. Only Ida Tarbell was "unconnected" to a specific club or organization.

The first issue the committee addressed was the developing food crisis. The group promoted planting vegetable gardens across the country and encouraged both drying foods (beans, peas, apples, for example) and canning vegetables and fruit. Knitting, bandage making, and sewing for the cause became important efforts.

During the war, women flocked into factories, taking their places as metal workers, machinists, and assembly line workers. Women replaced men who had already volunteered to serve in the military, yet there were still responsibilities at home for women with children. The Women's Committee urged women not working in factories to open daycare centers and support local schools.

Ida worked hard as a committee member, although her opinion was not always welcome. The committee's leaders—Dr. Anna Howard Shaw and Carrie Chapman Catt—were feminists and did not appreciate Tarbell's inconsistent attitude toward women's causes.

In 1918, with the war still going on, Ida Tarbell headed off on another one-town-per-day Chautauqua tour. This tour was very different from her first tour.

Women's rights leaders, such as Dr. Anna Howard Shaw, disliked Tarbell's conservative attitudes toward her own sex. *(Library of Congress)*

Then, war was a mere shadow, something that was happening far away from home. In 1918, war was the reality. Every town had men and women serving in the military. Every town had lost citizens, and gold stars hung in the windows of bereaved families.

Conversation was confined to one topic: World War I. Its battles, its sacrifices, the actions of heroes were told and retold in newspapers and on town corners. Ida found the stage that she spoke from was now draped in American flags. She herself was expected to wear a flag in place of a flower corsage.

When the war ended in 1918, the Women's Committee was quickly disbanded, and Ida was once again out of work. A new job opened for her with the *Red Cross Magazine.* Tarbell's long-time friend John Phillips was the magazine's editor, and he sent Ida off to France to write about the effects of the war there.

It occurred to Ida that France had suffered greatly under the German onslaught. When she packed for Paris, she brought with her chocolates, boots, blankets, socks, and sweaters in one case—and a gigantic ham in another! The trip by ship was easy, but traveling from the dock to Paris by train was not quite as successful.

Later, Ida related the story of her journey:

> In the long and tedious railroad journey form Bordeaux to Paris, I was packed in with a group of fine serious young Quakers going over to help a reconstruction project, and that terrible piece of luggage jumped from the rack and almost brained one of my

companions. I cannot recall all the adventures of that ham, but I know that I was never more relieved than when I laid it at the feet of my old friend [Madame Marillier].

Back in Paris, Ida found that she could almost relive her youth. She had expected that Paris would be on the verge of starving after the war, but discovered, instead, that food was plentiful, although very expensive. Eggs, milk, cheese, fresh vegetables, and bread were available—for a price. The best place to shop was the American Commissariat.

Grocery shopping among the Parisians provided Ida with more than food to eat. In the marketplace, she heard tales from average French citizens about their lives during the war and their expectations now that the war was over. Many French people felt that Germany and its allies should be forced to pay for the war.

Ida discovered that the war's effects in Paris were small, yet very real. Nothing had been painted since the start of the war. New buildings remained unbuilt; damaged structures stayed damaged. Museums had stored their best pieces or shipped them away for safety. Frames hung empty, awaiting the return of paintings that had passed the war in the south of France.

Outlying areas had suffered far more during the war than Paris. Many towns had been reduced to rubble. On trips into the country, Ida met people who were living amid the wreckage of their homes and farms. Some had little food to eat; others wore tattered clothes. Everyone

Ida met had a story of how they had survived, and Ida wrote those stories for her readers.

During that time, Ida wrote articles for the *Red Cross Magazine.* These articles included "The French Woman and Her New World," "The Homing Instinct of Woman," and "That Brave Northwest," all published in 1919. In these pieces, Tarbell tried to tell the American reader about the struggles, nobility, and hopes of the average French woman, returning to normal life after the war.

Chapter Nine

All in the Day's Work

Toward the end of the 1910s, Ida discovered that her brother Will had caused the family fortune serious damage. Local bankers had allowed Will to borrow against his inheritance, and Will was unable to repay his debts. Ida stepped in to pay the $10,000 he owed.

Ida suffered a physical breakdown in 1918, and was sent to Johns Hopkins Hospital in Maryland. She was rundown, severely underweight, and suffering from tuberculosis. This was before the discovery of antibiotics, and Ida's illness could only be cured through bed rest, a healthy diet, and elimination of all stress. The rest cure took three months, during which Ida ate six raw eggs daily, in addition to three balanced meals. The prolonged rest was a disaster for Tarbell, who depended on being able to work to support herself. For her, no work meant no money.

Even after Ida returned home, she complained of feeling weak, tired, and shaky. When her family doctor told her there was nothing wrong, she felt relieved. In fact, there was a great deal wrong—Ida was suffering from the early stages of Parkinson's disease. However, Dr. Brooks knew of no treatment for Parkinson's, so he told Ida to continue with life as usual.

As the Roaring Twenties began, Twin Oaks farm became Ida's main source of comfort. She worked in her garden, researched and wrote in the study, and provided a refuge for family members in need.

The Tarbell family needs were many. Ida's niece Clara and Clara's husband, Tristram Tupper, lived in a cottage on Twin Oaks. Clara's husband was at the start of a promising writing career, but the couple needed a place to live and money to live on. Sarah Tarbell, Ida's sister, resided nearby.

Will Tarbell suffered an emotional breakdown in 1924. Ida had to choose whether to have Will hospitalized or bring him and his wife, Ella, to live with her. Ida had always taken her family responsibilities seriously. She rearranged the household so that Will and Ella would have ample room, while Ida moved herself into a smaller bedroom downstairs.

With so many people to support, Ida needed money. She realized that the finances of a freelancer were irregular, but she believed that she could earn enough money if she worked hard. But more than money, Ida missed the daily association with other writers and editors her previous jobs provided. She said, "Giving up the salary troubled me less than finding myself without the regular professional contacts which I had so enjoyed for twenty years, and on which I found, now I was free, that I had come to depend more than I would have believed."

Tarbell set up an office at home in her study. She had a secretary—another person for Ida to support—and planned to revamp her history of Standard Oil. Unfortunately, there was no market for a rewrite of her original book. Still, Ida needed work. Early in 1924, an editor named Rutger Jewett contacted Ida to write the biography of Judge Elbert H. Gary, then chairman of the U.S. Steel Corporation. Tarbell was not interested. Instead, she signed on for another lecture tour for the fourth consecutive year. This time, however, Ida's poor health was her downfall. She was forced to return home and reconsider her position about the Gary biography.

At the beginning of the project, Tarbell went to Gary and told him that she really did not want to write about him. She recalled her relationship with Henry Rogers of Standard Oil and how that friendship fell apart as she dug deeper into his company's business practices. Nearing seventy, Ida did not want to go through that again.

Judge Gary assured her that if she found anything in U.S. Steel's business practices that she felt were either illegal or unethical, she should bring it to him. He had no wish to cover up wrong-doings, but to correct them.

Thus began the work that Ida Tarbell considered her most courageous, while her critics condemned her for being cowardly. The simple fact was that Gary had done an admirable job as the head of U.S. Steel. In her autobiography, Tarbell described Gary's efforts:

Orders went out neither to ask nor to accept special favors from the railroads. Full yearly reports of the financial condition of the Corporation, whether good or bad, were sent out. These reports reached the public as early as they did the directors themselves, putting an end to the advance information which many insiders were accustomed to using for stock selling or buying. Various forms of predatory competition were attacked from the inside. Judge Gary not only laid down his code, he followed it up, preached it zealously to his board.

Ida may not have wanted to write Gary's biography, but the money was excellent. She earned $10,000 for the book and an equal sum for the magazine serial rights. The cash would go far to support her family, as well as to pay off Will's debts.

By the time Gary's biography was published, Ida had grown quite fond of the judge. Critics, however, read the work and trashed her efforts. One review, entitled "The Taming of Ida Tarbell," accused her of falling in with her sworn enemy, big business. Said Ida, "I knew how it would be when I started. But I must confess that more than once, while I was carrying on my work, I shivered with distaste at the suspicion I knew I was bringing on myself. The only time in my professional life I feel I deserve to be called courageous was when I wrote the life of Judge Gary."

When Ida was one year shy of seventy, she received an assignment from *McCall's* magazine to write a series of articles on Benito Mussolini. In Italy, Mussolini had risen to fame as a general and a fascist dictator. By the mid-1920s, Mussolini had made great changes in Italy, some good and some bad.

Friends told Ida to expect the worst from Mussolini. They said he was rude, arrogant, and demanding. She was told that she could not expect to read foreign papers while in Italy because Mussolini had banned them. She was warned that she might be arrested. She was instructed to greet *Il Duce,* as Mussolini was called, using a fascist salute and to speak only in Italian. More importantly, *McCall's* said she would receive $25,000 for the series. Ida headed off to Italy.

All the warnings and forecasts of doom turned out to be rubbish. News kiosks throughout Rome carried newspapers in English and French, as well as Italian. Her bags were never searched, her papers were not seized, and her mail arrived unopened. During the months she stayed in Italy, Ida found the country beautiful and the people charming. She described her experience later in her biography:

> The first thing that springs to my mind now when I recall those months in Italy is a long procession of men, women, and children bent in labor. They harvested fields of rice, wheat, alfalfa, laying grain in perfect swaths; they sat on the ground, stripping and sorting tobacco leaves. Tiny girls, old women crowded narrow rooms, embroidering with sure fingers lovely designs on linen, fine and coarse; they cooked their meals before all the world in the narrow streets of Naples; they carried home at sunset from

the terraces or slopes of mountains great baskets of grapes, olives, lemons—young women straight and firm, their burdens poised surely on their heads, old women bent under the weight on their backs. They drove donkeys so laden that only a nodding head, a switching tail were visible; they filled the roads with their gay two-wheeled carts, tended sheep, ran machines, sat in markets, spun, weaved, molded, built—a world of work.

Ida's interview with Mussolini was another surprise. The man was gracious, welcoming. He spoke to her in French, knowing that her Italian was inferior. He was interested in his people, in providing them with better housing, better jobs, better lifestyles. They had a comfortable, cozy chat, and no one could have been more surprised than Ida Tarbell. Despite the negative reports that preceded him, Mussolini seemed to Ida to be kind, generous, and courteous. Nonetheless, for years she regularly expected to read of his assassination. She hoped that he would have the chance to bring about the changes he planned, yet she doubted they would come about.

Although they paid well, magazine articles were few and far between. There was no way for Ida to earn regular money except through lecture tours. Payment for a speaking tour was immediate. Between 1920 and 1932, Ida lectured every year. On her tours, she visited every state, saw every natural wonder, and every major city in the United States at that time.

Ida also took note of poverty in America in slums

Although she suffered from Parkinson's disease, Ida Tarbell continued to work into her eighties. *(Library of Congress)*

and Hoovervilles—towns erected on public land during the Great Depression and named for President Herbert Hoover. She saw empty towns, deserted when work was no longer available. She waited for trains along with people heading west, looking for farm work.

Throughout the years, the simple nature of the Chautauqua tent changed. In the early days, she walked on stage and spoke. Now, she became part of a spectacle—and she did not like it. At some places, she was introduced by an emcee, at others she became part of a pageant in which Ida and several others marched on stage amid fanfares and tributes. Occasionally, the stage was set with chairs and couches, and Ida would be joined by a group of local women behind a majestic curtain.

From these extensive tours, Ida developed two theories about living in the United States. The first was that people wanted to live according to what they believed were the national standards of the day. The second was that the trend to conform to national standards was blotting out the unique character of towns, cities, and regions. For Ida personally, the travels were uplifting, but exhausting. By 1932, she could no longer travel, no longer lecture at the pace required by the tours. It was time to head home.

Ida had planned to retire by the age of seventy, but there was much to be done. The need for money and the continuous desire to produce never left her. She said, "I consoled myself by saying, 'At seventy, you stop.' I planned for it. I would burrow into the country, have a microscope—my old love. I knew by this time that was not the way for me to find God, but I expected to have a lot of fun watching the Protozoa and less anguish than watching men and women."

At eighty, she was still at work. She completed *All In the Day's Work*, her autobiography, in 1939, at the age of eighty-two. The book met with mixed reviews. Her life story, the people she knew, the work she accomplished paled in comparison to the headlines that announced the start of yet another world war in Europe.

By then, Ida knew that she had Parkinson's disease and that her time was limited. Her hands shook dreadfully. She could no longer sit erect in a chair, and she walked with jerky, odd movements. In 1940, she closed her apartment in New York City. She could no longer travel back and forth, and there was no purpose in paying for an apartment that went empty month after month.

Ida stayed in Connecticut and began her next book, *Life After Eighty*. It was an effort she never finished. Just before Christmas 1943, Sarah Tarbell found Ida in bed in a coma. On January 6, 1944, Ida Minerva Tarbell died of pneumonia. She had requested that her body be returned to Titusville and buried in the family plot with her father, mother, and siblings. She left her home in Connecticut to Sarah and the lifetime collection of her papers to Allegheny College. The woman whose writing revolutionized journalism and spanned almost seventy years finally set down her pen.

Glossary

biography: (n.) a factual account of a person's life

corporation: (n.) a business in which many people are allowed to act as one

corruption: (n.) dishonesty, usually of public officials

dormitory: (n.) sleeping quarters for a large number of people

evolution: (n.) the theory of the development of plants and animals on Earth

freelance: (adj.) describes a writer, actor, or artist who sells work by contract rather than working for a specific company

investigative: (adj.) probes into an issue or topic

journalism: (n.) factual writing published in newspapers, magazines, or other media

kerosene: (n.) a petroleum product burned for heat or light

monopoly: (n.) exclusive control of a product or service by one company

muckraker: (n.) a person who investigates scandalous or illegal acts and makes them public preceptress: (n.) the head of a school

refining: (n.) processing a raw product to make it usable, such as sugarcane, oil, or iron ore

revolution: (n.) a change brought about by a political, military, or social group

rhetoric: (n.) speaking or writing effectively

scarlet fever: (n.) an infectious disease that mostly affects children, most notably recognized by a sore throat accompanied by a vivid red rash

suffrage: (n.) the right to vote

tariff: (n.) a tax on goods and services brought into a country

temperance: (n.) a social movement against drinking alcohol

trust: (n.) a group of corporations headed by a board of trustees

vigilante: (n.) a person who works outside the law to try to correct what he or she feels is an injustice

Timeline

1857—Born on November 5, Erie County, Pennsylvania.

1860—Family relocates to Rouseville.

1870—Family moves to Titusville, where Ida attends a regular school.

1876—Enters Allegheny College.

1880—Becomes Preceptress of Poland Seminary, Poland, Ohio.

1883—Joins the staff of the *Chautauquan*.

1891—Moves to Paris.

1894—Publishes biography of Napoleon in *McClure's*.

1902—*History of the Standard Oil Company* begins serial publication in *McClure's*.

1907—*He Knew Lincoln* published.

1911—*The Tariff in Our Times* published.

1919—*Red Cross Magazine* sends Ida to Paris after World War I ends.

1926—Interviews Mussolini and writes four articles about him for *McCall's*.

1939—Autobiography, *All in the Day's Work*, published.

1944—Dies after illness on January 6.

Sources

_____
_____

CHAPTER ONE—A Curious Mind

p. 10, "with its dozens of filled . . ." Ida Tarbell. *All In The Day's Work (*Boston: G.K. Hall, 1985,) p. 1.

p. 14, "My paramount . . ." Abraham Lincoln. Letter to Horace Greeley, August, 1862.

CHAPTER TWO—Knowledge and Independence

p. 18, "I remember best . . ." Kathleen Brady. *Ida Tarbell: Portrait of a Muckraker* (New York: Seaview/Putnam, 1984,) p. 23.

p. 20, "If Bentley Hall . . ." Tarbell, *Day's Work,* p. 41.

p. 21, "The quest for the truth . . ." Brady, *Muckraker*, p. 20.

p. 24, "A woman is a natural executive . . ." Tarbell, *Day's Work*, p. 73.

p. 26, "Three things worth knowing . . ." Ida Tarbell. "Women as Inventors," (Meadville, PA: *Chautauquan,* March, 1887,) p. 355.

p. 27, "You're not a writer . . ." Tarbell, *Day's Work,* p. 87.

CHAPTER THREE—Paris on a Shoestring

p. 29, ". . . we learned how to order . . ." Ibid., p. 91.

p. 31, "The blues and greens . . ." Ida Tarbell. Letter to her family. Tarbell Archives, Pelletier Library, Allegheny College, Meadville, PA, 1892.

p. 33, "A slender figure . . ." Tarbell, *Day's Work,* p. 119.

CHAPTER FOUR—Biographer

p. 42, "He was all Todd . . ." Tarbell, *Day's Work*, p. 166.

CHAPTER FIVE—Rockefeller and Standard Oil

p. 52, "a striking figure . . ." Tarbell, *Day's Work*, p. 212.

p. 57, "There was an awful age . . ." Ibid., p. 235-236.

p. 58, "With Mr. Rockefeller's genius." *The American Experience,* "The Rockefellers." http://www.pbs.org/wgbh/amex/rockefellers/

p. 58, "is simply covering up . . ." Ibid.

p. 60, "At the mention . . ." Ron Chernow. *Titan: The Life of John D. Rockefeller, Sr.* (New York: Random House, Inc., 1998,) p. 450.

CHAPTER SIX—Muckraker

p. 62, "The man who never . . ." Robert C. Kochersberger, Jr. *More Than a Muckraker.* (Knoxville: University of Tennessee Press,) 1994.

p. 65, "Things happened . . ." Tarbell, *Day's Work,* p. 263.

p. 69, "For years the death rate . . ." Ida Tarbell. "A Tariff-Made City," *American Magazine,* 1909.

p. 72, "Was it not the duty . . ." Ibid., p. 280.

p. 74, "The trouble's been . . ." Ibid., p. 289.

p. 76, "Every year over NINE . . ." Ida Tarbell. "The Floyd Collinses of Our Mines." Pelletier Library, Allegheny College, Meadville, PA, 1925?

CHAPTER SEVEN—The Business of Being a Woman

p. 78, "If one has proved herself capable . . ." Ida Tarbell. "Women in Journalism." (Meadville, PA: *Chautauquan,* April 1887,) p. 394.

p. 78, "The central fact . . ." Ida Tarbell. "The Business of Being a Woman." New York: Macmillan, 1912, p. 53.

p. 78, "I spent quite as much time . . ." Tarbell, *Day's Work,* p. 283

p. 79, "Feeling as I did . . ." Ibid., p. 327-328.

p. 80, "That title was like a red rag . . ." Ibid., p. 327

CHAPTER EIGHT—A World Gone Mad

p. 83, "I was free . . ." Tarbell, *Day's Work,* p. 300

p. 83, "He began by putting me . . ." Ibid., p. 301.

p. 85, "My first contribution . . ." Ibid., p. 319

p. 88, "In the long and tedious railroad journey . . ." Ibid., p. 337

CHAPTER NINE—All in the Day's Work

p. 92, "Giving up the salary . . ." Tarbell, *Day's Work,* p. 361.

p. 94, "Orders went out . . ." Ibid., p. 366.

p. 94, "I knew how it would be . . ." Ibid., p. 371.

p. 96, "The first thing that springs to my mind . . ." Ibid., pp. 380-381

p. 98, "I consoled myself . . ." Ibid., p. 398

Bibliography

American History Desk Reference. New York: Macmillan, 1997.

The American Experience, "The Rockefellers." Boston: Public Broadcasting System, 1999.

The Oxford Children's Book of Famous People. New York: Oxford University Press, 1999.

Brady, Kathleen. *Ida Tarbell, Portrait of a Muckraker.* New York: Seaview/Putnam, 1984.

Chernow, Ron. *Titan: The Life of John D. Rockefeller, Sr.* New York: Random House, Inc., 1998.

Conn, Frances G. *Ida Tarbell, Muckraker.* Nashville, Tennessee: Thomas Nelson, Inc., 1972.

Fleming, Alice. *Ida Tarbell, First of the Muckrakers.* New York: Thomas Y. Crowell, 1971.

Kochersberger, Robert C., Jr. *More Than a Muckraker.* Knoxville: University of Tennessee Press, 1994.

Lincoln, Abraham. In a letter to Horace Greeley, August, 1862.

Lyon, Peter. *Success Story: The Life and Times of S.S. McClure.* New York: Charles Scribner's Sons, 1963.

Paradis, Adrian A. *Ida M. Tarbell, Pioneer Woman Journalist and Biographer.* Chicago: Regensteiner Publishing Enterprises, Inc., 1985.

Schlesinger, Arthur M., Jr., ed. *The Almanac of American History.* New York: Barnes & Noble, 1993.

Tarbell, Ida M. A family letter. Tarbell Archives, Pelletier Library, Allegheny College, Meadville, PA, 1892.

————."A Tariff-Made City," New York: *The American Magazine,* 1909.

————. "Making a Man of Herself," New York: *The American Magazine,* February 1912.

————. "The Business of Being a Woman." New York: Macmillan, 1912.

————. "The Floyd Collinses of Our Mines." Pelletier Library, Allegheny College, Meadville, PA, 1925?

————. "Women as Inventors," Meadville, PA: *The Chautauquan,* March, 1887.

————. "Women in Journalism," Meadville, PA: *The Chautauquan,* April 1887.

————. *All In The Day's Work.* Boston: G.K. Hall, 1985.

————. *The Business of Being a Woman.* New York: Macmillan Co., 1914.

————. *The History of the Standard Oil Company.* New York: Macmillan Co., 1904.

————. "Tariff in Our Times," New York: *The American Magazine,* March 1909.

Websites

_____

Drake Well Museum, Titusville, Pennsylvania
www.drakewell.org/

The History of the Standard Oil Company by Ida Tarbell, transcribed by the University of Rochester
www.history.rochester.edu/fuels/tarbell/MAIN.HTM

Ida Tarbell Homepage at Alleghany College
www.tarbell.allegheny.edu

PBS American Experience: The Rockefellers
www.pbs.org/wgbh/amex/rockefellers/peopleevents/
p_tarbell.html

The Rockefeller Archive Center, Sleepy Hollow, New York
www.rockefeller.edu/archive.ctr/

Index